RIVER RIVER

OTHER BOOKS BY ARTHUR SZE

The Willow Wind
Two Ravens
Dazzled

RIVER RIVER

ARTHUR SZE

LOST ROADS PUBLISHERS
Number 31 Providence 1987

Grateful acknowledgement is made to the following publications in which some of these poems first appeared: *The Bloomsbury Review, Bridge, Cedar Rock, Contact II, Coyote's Journal, Floating Island, The Greenfield Review, Harvard Magazine, High Plains Literary Review, New Letters, El Palacio, Pax, River Styx, Sonora Review, Spazio Umano* (Milan), *Tendril, 2 Plus 2* (Lausanne), *Tyuonyi, Anthology of Magazine Verse & Yearbook of American Poetry,* and *Crossing the River.*

Library of Congress Cataloging in Publication Data

Sze, Arthur
River River / Arthur Sze

p. cm. – (Lost roads; no. 31)
ISBN 0-918786-35-5
I. Title.
PS3569.Z38R5 1987
811'.54 – dc19 87-17384
CIP

Published by Lost Roads Publishers
PO Box 5848
Providence, Rhode Island 02903
First Printing by McNaughton and Gunn
Second Printing March 1989 by McNaughton and Gunn
Typeset by Michael Sykes, Floating Island, Pt. Reyes
Cover print, *Song,* is by the late Japanese National Treasure, Keisuke Serizawa.
The author wishes to thank Mr. Chosuke Serizawa for copyright permission,
and Mr. Shinya Tokuyama for color positive film.
Book design by D.C. Wright and Forrest Gander.

This project is supported in part by a grant from the National Endowment for the Arts in Washington, D.C., a federal agency.

FOR MONA

CONTENTS

RIVER RIVER

THE LEAVES OF A DREAM ARE THE LEAVES OF AN ONION

1

Red oak leaves rustle in the wind.
Inside a dream, you dream the leaves
scattered on dirt, and feel it
as an instance of the chance configuration

to your life. All night you feel
red horses galloping in your blood,
hear a piercing siren, and are in love
with the inexplicable. You walk

to your car, find the hazard lights
blinking: find a rust-brown knife, a trout,
a smashed violin in your hands.
And then you wake, inside the dream,

to find tangerines ripening in the silence.
You peel the leaves of the dream
as you would peel the leaves off an onion.
The layers of the dream have no core,

no essence. You find a tattoo of
a red scorpion on your body.
You simply laugh, shiver in the frost,
and step back into the world.

2

A Galapagos turtle has nothing to do
with the world of the neutrino.
The ecology of the Galapagos Islands
has nothing to do with a pair of scissors.
The cactus by the window has nothing to do
with the invention of the wheel.
The invention of the telescope
has nothing to do with a red jaguar.
No. The invention of the scissors
has everything to do with the invention of the telescope.
A map of the world has everything to do
with the cactus by the window.
The world of the quark has everything to do
with a jaguar circling in the night.
The man who sacrifices himself and throws a Molotov
cocktail at a tank has everything to do
with a sunflower that bends to the light.

3

Open a window and touch the sun,
or feel the wet maple leaves flicker in the rain.
Watch a blue crab scuttle in clear water,
or find a starfish in the dirt.
Describe the color green to the color blind,
or build a house out of pain.

The world is more than you surmise.
Take the pines, green-black, slashed by light,
etched by wind, on the island
across the riptide body of water.
Describe the thousand iridescent needles
to a blind albino Tarahumara.

In a bubble chamber, in a magnetic field,
an electron spirals and spirals in to the center,
but the world is more than such a dance:
a spiraling in to the point of origin,
a spiraling out in the form of a
wet leaf, a blue crab, or a green house.

4

The heat ripples ripple the cactus.
Crushed green glass in a parking lot
or a pile of rhinoceros bones
give off heat, though you might not notice it.

The heat of a star can be measured
under a spectrometer, but not
the heat of the mind, or the heat of Angkor Wat.
And the rubble of Angkor Wat

gives off heat; so do apricot blossoms
in the night, green fish, black bamboo,
or a fisherman fishing in the snow.
And an angstrom of shift turns the pleasure

into pain. The ice that rips the fingerprint
off your hand gives off heat;
and so does each moment of existence.
A red red leaf, disintegrating in the dirt,

burns with the heat of an acetylene flame.
And the heat rippling off
the tin roof of the adobe house
is simply the heat you see.

5

What is the secret to a Guarneri violin?
Wool dipped in an indigo bath turns bluer
when it oxidizes in the air. Marat is
changed in the minds of the living.
A shot of tequila is related to Antarctica
shrinking. A crow in a bar or red snapper on ice
is related to the twelve tone method
of composition. And what does the tuning of tympani
have to do with the smell of your hair?
To feel, at thirty, you have come this far –
to see a bell over a door as a bell
over a door, to feel the care and precision
of this violin is no mistake, nor is the
sincerity and shudder of passion by which you live.

6

Crush an apple, crush a possibility.
No single method can describe the world;
therein is the pleasure
of chaos, of leaps in the mind.
A man slumped over a desk in an attorney's office
is a parrot fish caught in a seaweed mass.
A man who turns to the conversation in a bar
is a bluefish hooked on a cigarette.
Is the desire and collapse of desire in an unemployed carpenter
the instinct of salmon to leap upstream?
The smell of eucalyptus can be incorporated
into a theory of aggression.
The pattern of interference in a hologram
replicates the apple, knife, horsetails on the table,
but misses the sense of chaos, distorts
in its singular view. Then
touch, shine, dance, sing, be, becoming, be.

19

THE APHRODISIAC

"Power is my aphrodisiac."
Power enables him to
connect a candle-lit dinner
to the landing on the moon.
He sees a plot in the acid
content of American soil,
malice in a configuration
of palm leaf shadows.
He is obsessed with
the appearance of democracy
in a terrorized nation.
If the price of oil
is an owl claw, a nuclear
reactor is a rattlesnake
fang. He has no use
for the song of an oriole,
bright yellow wings.
He refuses to consider
a woman in a wheelchair
touching the shadow of
a sparrow, a campesino
dreaming of spring.
He revels in the instant
before a grenade explodes.

THE ANSEL ADAMS CARD

You left a trail of bad checks in forty six states.
When you were finally arrested on a check for $36.10,
you no longer knew how many aliases you had burned
out. You simply knew you had waited too long at the checkout
counter. The police found five sets of current driver
licenses in your car, titles to ten other cars,
two diamond rings, and $2500 cash.

You started by running off with an ex-convict,
forging your mother's signature at the post office,
collecting her mail, and cashing a check.
You bought a car and groceries with the check:
took off, then, to Chicago. The scenario
was to open a checking account for $50,
withdraw $40 at the end of the day, and use the blank
checks to shop with. Again and again: how many
times until you saw your signature at the checkout counter?
Once, you thought quickly, pulled out a license
with a different name, ran out to your husband
waiting in the car.

And he was scot-free: a tattoo of white lightning
on his arms. Now he is a used car salesman in Kansas City –
forging car titles and duplicating sales?
I see you as a green leaf in sunshine
after a rain. If you are paroled in July,
what will happen? Surely you won't forget life in prison,
jumping bail, on the run, the rape, the humiliation,
the arrest? But you are walking on glass.
You are now married to an inmate in Texarkana.
I give you this Ansel Adams card with one aspen, leafy,
against a forest, one aspen bright in the sun.

NEW WAVE

He listens to a punk rock group,
Dead on Arrival,
on his miniature Sony headphones and cassette recorder.
With the volume turned up,
the noise of the world
can't touch him.
No one's going to tell *him* what to do:
whether to drive
his car up an arroyo,
or wire the house with explosives.
He's given us the rap
on New Wave:
how it's noise and is disgusting—
though we suspect
whatever he dislikes is New Wave.
His mind is a Geiger counter bombarded with radiation:
the clusters of
click click click click, click click
a daily dose of carcinogens
without which
it would be impossible to live.
He watches us listen to a Jewish astrologer
reading a horoscope,
and glances out the window.
Now he flips
the cassette and turns up the volume.
I can see the headlines now:
Juvenile Detonates House,
pleads temporary insanity
due to the effects of listening to Agent Orange.

EVERY WHERE AND EVERY WHEN

1

Catch a moth in the Amazon; pin it under glass.
See the green-swirling magenta-flecked wings

miming a fierce face. And dead, watch it fly.
Throw a piece of juniper into a fire.

Search out the Odeon in Zurich to find Lenin or Klee.
No one has a doctrine of recollection to

bring back knowledge of what was, is?
The Odeon cafe is not the place to look

for Lenin's fingerprint. The piece of burning juniper
has the sound of the bones of your hands

breaking. And the moth at the window, magenta-flecked,
green-swirling, is every where and every when.

2

Everything is supposed to fit: mortise and tenon,
arteries and veins, hammer, anvil, stirrup in the ear,

but it does not fit. Someone was executed
today. Tomorrow friends of the executed will execute

the executers. And this despair is the intensifying
fever and chill, in shortening intervals,

of a malaria patient. Evil is not a variety of
potato found in the Andes. The smell of a gardenia

is not scissors and sponge in the hands of
an inept surgeon. Everything is supposed to fit:

but wander through Cuzco and the orientation of
streets and plazas is too Spanish. Throw

hibiscus on a corpse. Take an aerial view;
see the city built in the shape of a jaguar's head.

3

I pick a few mushrooms in the hills,
but do not know the lethal from the edible.

I cannot distinguish red wool dyed
with cochineal or lac, but know that

cochineal with alum, tin, salt and lime juice
makes a rosé, a red, a burgundy.

Is it true an anti-matter particle
never travels as slow as the speed of light,

and, colliding with matter, explodes?
The mind shifts as the world shifts.

I look out the window, watch Antares glow.
The world shifts as the mind shifts;

or this belief, at least, increases
the pleasure of it all – the smell of espresso

in the street, picking blueberries,
white-glazed, blue-black,

sieved gold from a river, this moment
when we spin and shine.

THE REHEARSAL

Xylophone, triangle, marimba, soprano, violin –
the musicians use stop watches, map out
in sound the convergence of three rivers at a farm,

but it sounds like the jungle at midnight.
Caught in a blizzard and surrounded by wolves
circling closer and closer, you might

remember the smell of huisache on a warm spring night.
You might remember three deer startled and stopped
at the edge of a road in a black canyon.

A child wants to act crazy, acts crazy,
is thereby sane. If you ache with longing
or are terrified: ache, be terrified, be hysterical;

walk into a redwood forest and listen:
hear a pine cone drop into a pool of water.
And what is your life then? In the time

it takes to make a fist or open your hand,
the musicians have stopped. But a life only stops
when what you want is no longer possible.

KAYAKING AT NIGHT ON TOMALES BAY

Kayak on the black water,
and feel a gold feather float in the air.
Pick up a red shard in the dirt,
and feel someone light a
candle and sing.

A man may die crashing into a redwood house,
or die as someone pries
open an oyster.
A kayaker may hit a rock, and
drown at the bottom of a waterfall.

Is the world of the dead
a world of memory? Or a world of ten dimensions?
Calculate the number of
configurations to a tangram?
Compute the digits of pi?

Kayak on the black water,
and feel the moonlight glisten the pines.
Drift, drift, and drifting:
the lights of cars on the road take a
thousand years to arrive.

MISTAKING WATER HEMLOCK FOR PARSLEY

Mistaking water hemlock for parsley,
I die two hours
later in the hospital;
or I turn the shish kebab on the hibachi,
and reel, crash
to the floor, die of a ruptured aorta.

Then you place an ear of blue corn
in my left hand,
tie a single turkey feather
around my right ankle.
I hear the coffin nailed shut,
hear green singing finches in the silence.

And in the silence I float on water,
feel an equilibrium,
feel the gravitational pull of the universe
slow everything down
and begin to draw everything back
to the center.

Then a star is a taste of olives,
a sun the shine on the black wings of ravens.
I wake, and joy and love, and feel
each passion makes me,
protean, wiser, stronger.
I want to live and live and live and live.

EVIL GRIGRI

Evil grigri:
taste acid in the word *sybaritic.*
Feel deer antlers polished in rain and sun;
taste green almonds,
the polar ice cap of Mars melting at the tip of your tongue.

Is it possible to wake
dressed in a tuxedo smoking a cigarette staring at a firing squad?
A man is cursed
when he remembers he cannot remember his dream;
taste sugar in the word *voluptuous;*
feel a macaw feather brush across your closed eyelids.

See the dead laugh at the pile of shoes at Dachau.
See as a man with one eye
the dead alive and singing,
walking down the equinoctial axis of the midnight street.

Now feel how the ocarina of your body
waits for pleasure to blow and make an emerald sound in the air;
make an apotropaic prayer
that the day's evil become the day's wild thyme:

say guava-passionflower-hibiscus salt,
say sun-sea wave,
say wind-star, venom-night,
say mango-river, eucalyptus-scented fang.

THE PULSE

A woman in a psychiatric ward
is hysterical; she has to get a letter
to God by tomorrow or

the world will end. Which root
of a chiasma grows and grows?
Which dies? An analysis of

the visual cortex of the brain
confines your world-view even as you
try to enlarge it? I walk

down an arroyo lined with old tires
and broken glass, feel a pulse,
a rhythm in silence, a slow

blooming of leaves. I know
it is unlikely, but feel I could
find the bones of a whale

as easily as a tire iron.
I shut my eyes, green water flowing
in the acequia never returns.

THE DIAMOND POINT

Use the diamond point of grief:
incise a clear hibiscus in the windowpane.
A child picks apples in autumn light;
five minutes resemble a day?
But an aquamarine instant dropped
into water makes an entire pool shine.
Do you feel the forsythia about to explode?
The flow in a dead seal washed to shore?
I see the sloping street
to your house, bird of paradise in bloom:

silence when you lift the receiver off the phone,
shaft of spring light when you say "hello."
I see you smile in a flower dress –
intense pain, intense joy – waving goodbye,
goodbye, goodbye, goodbye, goodbye
1947, 1960, 1967, 1972, 1981.
A firework explodes in a purple chrysanthemum:
ooh and aah and then, then
use the diamond point of grief:
incise a clear hibiscus in the windowpane.

METASTASIS

Noon summer solstice light shines on a creation spiral petroglyph.
We stare up at a pictograph of a left hand,
a new moon, a supernova of 1054 A.D.
I dream of touching a rattlesnake,
want to find a fossil
of a green ginkgo leaf here in Chaco Wash.
I have not forgotten the death of Josephine Miles,
but forget grief,
that fried tripe;
I want to hike the thousand summer trails,
become sun, moon.
A rattlesnake slides into a coil:
if grief, grief, if pain, pain, if joy, joy.
In a night rain
all the emotions of a day become pure and shining.
I think, I no longer think:
metastasis: noon summer solstice light: turpentine, rags:
the new leaves of a peach delicate
and of light green hue.

HORSE FACE

A man in prison is called horse face, but does nothing
when everyone in the tailor shop has sharp cold scissors;

he remembers the insult but laughs it off. Even as he
laughs, a Cattaraugus Indian welding a steel girder

turns at a yell which coincides with the laugh and slips
to his death. I open a beer; a car approaches a garage.

The door opens, a light comes on, inside rakes gleam;
a child with dysentery washes his hands in cow piss.

I find a trail of sawdust, walk in a dead killer's
hardened old shoes, and feel how difficult it is to

sense the entire danger of a moment: a horse gives birth
to a foal, power goes out in the city, a dancer

stops in the dark and listening for the noise that was scored
in the performance hears only sudden panicked yells.

THE NEGATIVE

A man hauling coal in the street is stilled forever.
Inside a temple, instead of light

a slow shutter lets the darkness in.
I see a rat turn a corner running from a man with a chair trying to smash it,

see people sleeping at midnight in a Wuhan street on bamboo beds,
a dead pig floating, bloated, on water.

I see a photograph of a son smiling who two years ago fell off a cliff
and his photograph is in each room of the apartment.

I meet a woman who had smallpox as a child, was abandoned by her mother
but who lived, now has two daughters, a son, a son-in-law;

they live in three rooms and watch a color television.
I see a man in blue work clothes whose father was a peasant

who joined the Communist party early but by the time of the
    Cultural Revolution
had risen in rank and become a target of the Red Guards.

I see a woman who tried to kill herself with an acupuncture needle
but instead hit a vital point and cured her chronic asthma.

A Chinese poet argues that the fundamental difference between East and West
is that in the East an individual does not believe himself

in control of his fate but yields to it.
As a negative reverses light and dark

these words are prose accounts of personal tragedy becoming metaphor,
an emulsion of silver salts sensitive to light,

laughter in the underground bomb shelter converted into a movie theater,
lovers in the Summer Palace park.

WASABI

Quinine is to cinchona
as pain is to nerves? No,
as the depletion of ozone is to a city? No,

like a DNA double helix,
the purity of intention
is linked to the botched attempt.

The zing of a circular saw
is linked in time to
the smell of splintery charred plywood dust.

And the scent of red ginger
to a field guide is as
a blueprint to walking out of sunlight

into a cool stone Lama temple?
The mind at chess,
the mind at *go:* here

the purpose is not to prevail,
but to taste – as *ikebana*
is to spring cherry blossoms – *wasabi.*

THE SOLDERER

I watch a man soldering positive and negative speaker
wires to a plug inhale tin-lead alloy smoke.

He does not worry about a shift in the solar wind.
He does not worry about carcinogens.

Is his mind and memory as precise as his hands?
To suffer and suffer is not a necessary and sufficient

condition for revelation; open up a box of
Balinese flowers, roots, bark: the history of civilization

is to know you do not know what to do.
In my mind I practice rubbing a bronze spouting bowl

with both hands. The bowl begins to hum
and a standing wave makes the water splash up into my face.

I am stunned to hear a man who wore a T-shirt
with a silk-screened tie shot himself and is in critical

condition in the hospital. No one wants to
die suspended in air like gold dust flecked by sunlight.

RENGA

We hunger for the iridescent shine of an abalone shell

Stare at a newspaper, see the latest terrors

Want the sound of hail on a tin roof to reverberate forever

Want to feel the echo as we wash a rag, pick broccoli, sneeze

The sound does not make us forget the terrors

But the terrors are lived then as water in a stream

We hold, as in a tea ceremony, a bowl with both hands

Turn it a quarter turn, and another, and another

And when we see the green stillness

See the abalone shine, abalone shine

TEN THOUSAND TO ONE

The Phoenicians guarded a recipe that required
ten thousand murex shells to make
an ounce of Tyrian purple.

Scan the surface of Aldebaran with a radio wave;
grind lapis lazuli
into ultramarine.

Search the summer sky for an Anasazi turkey constellation;
see algae under an electron microscope
resemble a Magellanic cloud.

A chemist tried to convert benzene into quinine,
but blundered into a violet
aniline dye instead.

Have you ever seen maggots feed on a dead rat?
Listen to a red-tailed hawk glide
over the hushed spruce and

pines in a canyon. Feel a drop of water roll
down a pine needle, and glisten,
hanging, at the tip.

TO A COMPOSER

Red chair, blue chair, white chair, big chair, chair.
No, this is not the taste
of unripe persimmons,
nor standing on a New York street in December inhaling shish kebab smoke.
The dissonant seconds played on a piano
become macaws perched on cages.
A green Amazon parrot with yellow-tipped wings
lands on your shoulder.
The background hum
of loudspeakers becomes a humid environment.
You may open this door and walk into the aviary
when you least expect to,
startled walk on redwood planks over huge-leafed tropical plants
as a red-billed toucan flaps by.
Dirty utensils are piled in the sink,
coffee grinds clog the drain.
So what if the plumber pouring sulfuric acid
gives you a look
when you open the refrigerator
and pull out a just solidified chocolate turkey in a pan?
This is not 5:14 sharpening a pencil
but inhaling deeply and feeling the stream of air poured out through
    a *shakuhachi*
become a style of living.

SHOOTING STAR

1

In a concussion,
the mind severs the pain:
you don't remember flying off a motorcycle,
and landing face first
in a cholla.

But a woman stabbed in her apartment,
by a prowler searching for
money and drugs,
will never forget her startled shriek
die in her throat,
blood soaking into the floor.

The quotidian violence of the world
is like a full moon rising over the Ortiz mountains;
its pull is everywhere.
But let me live a life of violent surprise
and startled joy. I want to
thrust a purple iris into your hand,
give you a sudden embrace.

I want to live as Wang Hsi-chih lived
writing characters in gold ink on black silk –
not to frame on a wall,
but to live the splendor now.

2

Deprived of sleep, she hallucinated
and, believing she had sold the genetic
research on carp, signed a confession.
Picking psilocybin mushrooms in the mountains

of Veracruz, I hear tin cow bells
in the slow rain, see men wasted on pulque
sitting under palm trees. Is it
so hard to see things as they truly are:

a route marked in red ink on a map,
the shadows of apricot leaves thrown
in wind and sun on a wall? It is
easy to imagine a desert full of agaves

and golden barrel cactus, red earth, a red sun.
But to truly live one must see things
as they are, as they might become:
a wrench is not a fingerprint

on a stolen car, nor baling wire
the undertow of the ocean. I may hallucinate,
but see the men in drenched clothes
as men who saw and saw and refuse to see.

3

Think of being a judge or architect
or trombonist, and do not worry whether
thinking so makes it so. I overhear
two men talking in another room;

I cannot transcribe the conversation
word for word, but know if they are
vexed or depressed, joyful or nostalgic.
An elm leaf floats on a pond.

Look, a child wants to be a cardiologist
then a cartographer, but wanting so
does not make it so. It is not
a question of copying out the Heart Sutra

in your own blood on an alabaster wall.
It is not a question of grief or joy.
But as a fetus grows and grows,
as the autumn moon ripens the grapes,

greed and cruelty and hunger for power
ripen us, enable us to grieve, act,
laugh, shriek, see, see it all as
the water on which the elm leaf floats.

4

Write out the memories of your life
in red-gold disappearing ink, so that it all
dies, no lives. Each word you speak
dies, no lives. Is it all
at once in the mind? I once stepped
on a sea urchin, used a needle to dig out
the purple spines; blood soaked my hands.
But one spine was left, and I carried
it a thousand miles. I saw then
the olive leaves die on the branch,
saw dogs tear flesh off a sheep's corpse.
To live at all is to grieve;
but, once, to have it all at once
is to see a shooting star: shooting star
shooting star.

THE SILENCE

We walk through a yellow-ocher adobe house:
the windows are smeared with grease,
the doors are missing. Rain leaks
through the ceilings of all the rooms,
and the ribs of saguaro thrown across *vigas*
are dark, wet, and smell. The view outside
of red-faded and turquoise-faded adobes
could be Chihuahua, but it isn't.
I stop and look through an open doorway,
see wet newspapers rotting in mud
in the small center patio.
I suddenly see red bougainvillea blooming
against a fresh white-washed wall,
smell yellow wisteria through an open
window on a warm summer night;
but, no, a shot of cortisone is no cure
for a detaching retina. I might just
as well see a smashed dog in the street,
a boojum tree pushing its way up
through asphalt. And as we turn
and arrive where we began, I notice
the construction of the house is
simply room after room forming a square.
We step outside, and the silence is as
water is, taking the shape of the container.

KEOKEA

Black wattles along the edge of the clearing
below the house; a few koa plants are fenced in.

An old horse nibbles grass near the loquat tree.
Sunburned from hiking twelve miles into a volcano,

I do not know what I am looking at. Koa?
I want to walk into an empty charred house

and taste a jacaranda blossom.
Here Sun Yat-sen pounded his fist, sold opium,

dreamed the Chinese Revolution until blood broke
inside his brain? Marvin Miura is running

for political office; he wants aquaculture
for Maui, a ti leaf wrapped around a black river

stone, and he may get it. But one needs
to walk into a charred house where the sensuous

images of the world can be transformed. Otherwise
we can sit up all night on the redwood decking,

argue greed and corruption, the price of sugar cane,
how many pearls Imelda Marcos owns.

EARLY AUTUMN

I almost squashed a tarantula on the road.
And once when I found
earthstars growing under pines

almost sliced one open
but stopped.
The Mayans keyed their lives to the motion of Venus

but timing is human not Hegelian.
A revolutionary never waits
for cities to arrive

at appropriate orthodox Marxist conditions
to act.
A man used a chain saw

to cut yellow cedar,
but when he finished
discovered a minus tide had beached his skiff.

I've lived 12,680 days
and dreamed gold plankton flashing in my hands.
It flashes now

as I watch
red dragonflies vanish over water.
A blue tarantula crossed highway 286.

NOTHING CAN HEAL THE SEVERED NERVES OF A HAND?

Nothing can heal the severed nerves of a hand?
No one can stop feeling the touch of things
as the nerves die? A wasp lands on a yellow
but still green-veined leaf floating on water –
two dead flies drift aside. An old man
draws a llama on roller skates, remembers
arguing cases in court, now argues in a wheelchair
with whoever arrives. The nurses hate him,
but forget a life lived without mallet and chisel
is lived without scars. Then think how long
it takes the body to heal, the mind to shine.
An acupuncturist pushes a needle into your ear;
you incandesce. Yes. Yes, more, all, no, less, none.
Prune the branches of a pear at midnight;
taste a pine needle on a branch without touching it;
feel a seed germinate in the dark, sending
down roots, sending up leaves, ah!

SPLASH, FLOW

The unerring tragedy of our lives is to sail
a papyrus sailboat across the Atlantic ocean,

discover corn fossils in China: splash, flow.
When the bones of a platypus are found at Third Mesa,

the *koyemsi* will laugh. Watch a papyrus sailboat
slowly sink into the Mediterranean;

feel how grief, like a mordant, quietly attaches
pain to your nerves. *Now* splash, flow:

taste the sunrise shining inside your hands,
be jalapeño, wine, salt, gold, fire;

rejoice as your child finds a *malodorous lepiota*
under myrtle, smell the sea at night

as you hold the woman you love in your arms.

48

THE MOMENT OF CREATION

A painter indicates the time of day
in a still life: afternoon light slants on a knife,
lemons, green wine bottle with some red wine.
We always leave something unfinished?
We want x and having x want y and having y want z?
I try to sense the moment of creation
in the shine on a sliced lemon. I want to
connect throwing gravel on mud to being hungry.
"Eat," a man from Afghanistan said
and pointed to old rotting apples in the opened car trunk.
I see a line of men dancing a cloud dance;
two women dance intricate lightning steps
at either end. My mistakes and failures
pulse in me even as moments of joy,
but I want the bright moments to resonate out
like a gamelan gong. I want to make
the intricate tessellated moments of our lives
a floor of jade, obsidian, turquoise, ebony, lapis.

FORGET FEZ

Algol, Mizar:
I wanted to become pure like the Arabic
names of stars,

but perhaps I have erred.
At sunrise

the song of an ordinary robin startles me.
I want to say vireo,

but it *is* a robin.
In bed I turn and breathe
with your breath,

remember four days ago opening my hands
to a man who blessed me

and others with an eagle feather.
Betelgeuse, Deneb:

moonshine on a clear summer night,
but the splendor
is to taste smoke in your hair.

Forget Fez.

SHUTTLE

She is making stuffing for the turkey;
a few pistachio shells are on the kitchen table.
He looks out the window at the thermometer,

but sees a winter melon with a white glaze
in a New York Chinatown store at night.
Large sea bass swim in a tank by the window;

there are delicate blue crabs in a can
climbing and climbing on each other to get out.
She is thinking of a tapestry of red horses

running across a Southwestern landscape
with blue mesas in the distance. A shuttle goes
back and forth, back and forth through

the different sheds. He is talking to a man
who photographs empty parks in New York,
sees the branches of a black magnolia in early December.

She is washing out yarn so it will pack
and cover the warp; perhaps the tension
isn't right; the texture of Churro fleece

makes her hands tingle; a pot of walnuts
boils on the stove. He turns on the radio,
and listening to Nigerian music

feels the rumble of a subway under the floor,
feels the warmth of his hands
as he watches the snow fall and fall.

51

THROWING SALT ON A PATH

I watch you throw salt on the path,
and see abalone divers point to the sun,
discuss the waves, then throw their

gear back into the car. I watch you
collect large flakes of salt off rocks,
smell sliced ginger and fresh red

shrimp smoking over a fire. Ah,
the light of a star never stops, but travels
at the expanding edge of the universe.

A Swiss gold watch ticks and ticks;
but when you cannot hear it tick anymore,
it turns transparent in your hand.

You see the clear gold wheels
with sharp minute teeth catching each
other and making each spin.

The salt now clears a path in the snow,
expands the edges of the universe.

EDNA BAY

One day the men pulled a house off float logs
up on land with a five ton winch and a system of pulleys,
while a woman with a broken tooth chewed aspirin

and watched. A man was cutting down a red cedar
with a chain saw when it kicked back in his face,
cut his chin and hand to bone. A neighbor called Ketchikan

through a marine operator and chartered a plane
out before dark. Life on Kosciusko Island
is run by the weather and tides. Is the rain today

from the southeast or southwest? If southeast,
the men go into the rain forest cursing:
it will be hard to dig out pilings for a house.

I see how these fishermen hate seiners and humpies,
want to spend days and days trolling at twenty four fathoms.
I watch a great blue heron knife herring at low tide,

see a bald eagle circle and circle the shoreline.
One night with the full moon and a wind
on my face, I went across the bay in a skiff

looking at the rippling black water.
Days I will wake startled dreaming of bear,
see sheets of thin ice floating out in the bay.

BLACK JAVA PEPPER

Despair, anger, grief:
as a seiner indiscriminately hauls
humpies, jellyfish, kelp,
we must – farouche,

recalcitrant – conversely
angle for sockeye.
Our civilization has no genetic code
to make wasps return

each spring to build a nest
by the water heater
in the shed. We must – igneous,
metamorphic – despite

such plans as to push Mt. Fuji into the ocean
to provide more land –
grind cracked black
Java pepper into our speech

so that – limestone into marble,
granite into gneiss –
we become through our griefs –
rain forest islands – song.

THE HALIBUT

Dipping spruce branches into the calm water
to collect herring eggs
is an azure unthinking moment.
A fisherman never forgets the violet hue of December stars.
Does time make memory or memory make time polychromatic?
Squawk.
In a split second one hears a Stellar's jay, raven,
car tires on gravel, chain saw, fly, wind chime.
This constellation of polychromatic sounds
becomes a crimson moment
that fugitive colored will fade.
But one never forgets lighting kerosene lamps before noon.
In July when one has twenty hours of light
each second is fuchsia dyed.
One might be pouring Clorox down a hose to flush out an octopus
when one feels the moment explode,
when a fisherman using power crank and long line
looks into the water and sees
rising a two hundred pound halibut with bulging eyes.

STANDING ON AN ALDER BRIDGE OVER A CREEK

At low tide, midnight, with a flashlight,
we walk along the shore stumbling
on rocks, slightly drunk, step

through a creek where arctic water pours in
over my boots; nothing to do but
go on. We come to a tidal pool,

stop, see the exposed colonies of blue-black
mussels, go up to a trail, come
to an alder bridge; stop:

let the mature mind consider danger,
guess the architecture of a Persian house
in a dream contains the sockeye

an osprey hungers for. If so,
then emerald *if:* no, despair?
Like the camouflage of snowy plover eggs

in sand and bright sunshine,
we stand on an alder bridge over a creek,
are the April starlight and laugh.

HERE

Here a snail on a wet leaf shivers and dreams of spring.
Here a green iris in December.
Here the topaz light of the sky.
Here one stops hearing a twig break and listens for deer.
Here the art of the ventriloquist.
Here the obsession of a kleptomaniac to steal red pushpins.
Here the art of the alibi.
Here one walks into an abandoned farmhouse and hears a tarantella.
Here one dreamed a bear claw and died.
Here a humpback whale leaped out of the ocean.
Here the outboard motor stopped but a man made it to this island with one oar.
Here the actor forgot his lines and wept.
Here the art of prayer.
Here marbles, buttons, thimbles, dice, pins, stamps, beads.
Here one becomes terrified.
Here one wants to see as a god sees and becomes clear amber.
Here one is clear pine.

PARALLAX

"Kwakwha."
"Askwali."
The shift in Hopi when a man or woman says "thank you"
becomes a form of parallax.
A man travels

from Mindanao to Kyushu and says his inner geography
is enlarged by each new place.
Is it?
Might he not grow more by staring for twenty four hours
at a single pine needle?

I watch a woman tip an ashtray and empty
a few ashes into her mouth,
but ah, I want
other soliloquies.
I want equivalents to Chu-ko Liang sending his fire ships

downstream into Ts'ao Ts'ao's fleet.
It does not mean
a geneticist must quit
and devote his life to the preservation of rhinoceros,
but it might mean

watching a thousand snow geese drift on water
as the sky darkens minute by minute.
"Kwakwha,"
"askwali,"
whenever, wherever.

THE DAY CAN BECOME A ZEN GARDEN OF RAKED SAND

The day can become a Zen garden of raked sand
or a yellow tanager singing on a branch;

feel the terrors and pleasures of the morning:
in Tianjin all the foreigners are sent to a movie

and they must guess at what the authorities
do not wish them to see; dream a rainy landscape:

the Jemez Mountains breaking up in mist and jagged light
into a series of smaller but dazzling ranges;

to distinguish the smell of calendula from delphinium
is of no apparent consequence, but guess that

crucial moments in history involve an unobtrusive
point flaring into a startling revelation;

now be alive to the flowering chives by the window;
feel the potato plant in the whiskey barrel soak up sun;

feel this riparian light,
this flow where no word no water is.

THE UNNAMABLE RIVER

1

Is it in the anthracite face of a coal miner,
crystallized in the veins and lungs of a steel
worker, pulverized in the grimy hands of a railroad engineer?
Is it in a child naming a star, coconuts washing
ashore, dormant in a volcano along the Rio Grande?

You can travel the four thousand miles of the Nile
to its source and never find it.
You can climb the five highest peaks of the Himalayas
and never recognize it.
You can gaze through the largest telescope
and never see it.

But it's in the capillaries of your lungs.
It's in the space as you slice open a lemon.
It's in a corpse burning on the Ganges,
in rain splashing on banana leaves.

Perhaps you have to know you are about to die
to hunger for it. Perhaps you have to go
alone into the jungle armed with a spear
to truly see it. Perhaps you have to
have pneumonia to sense its crush.

But it's also in the scissor hands of a clock.
It's in the precessing motion of a top
when a torque makes the axis of rotation describe a cone:
and the cone spinning on a point gathers
past, present, future.

2

In a crude theory of perception, the apple you
see is supposed to be a copy of the actual apple,
but who can step out of his body to compare the two?
Who can step out of his life and feel
the Milky Way flow out of his hands?

An unpicked apple dies on a branch;
that is all we know of it.
It turns black and hard, a corpse on the Ganges.
Then go ahead and map out three thousand miles of the Yangtze;
walk each inch, feel its surge and
flow as you feel the surge and flow in your own body.

And the spinning cone of a precessing top
is a form of existence that gathers and spins death and life into one.
It is in the duration of words, but beyond words –
river river river, river river.
The coal miner may not know he has it.
The steel worker may not know he has it.
The railroad engineer may not know he has it.
But it is there. It is in the smell
of an avocado blossom, and in the true passion of a kiss.

ABOUT THE AUTHOR

Arthur Sze is a second-generation Chinese American who was born in New York City in 1950. He graduated from the University of California at Berkeley, and is the author of three other books of poetry and translations from the Chinese. He is the recipient of The Eisner Prize, UC Berkeley, three NEA Writers-in-Residence Grants, two Witter Bynner Foundation for Poetry Grants, and an NEA Creative Writing Fellowship. He has worked in the New Mexico and Alaska Artist-in-Residence programs, lives in Santa Fe, and currently teaches at the Institute of American Indian Arts.

ALSO FROM LOST ROADS

POETRY

Ralph Adamo, *The End Of The World; Sadness At The Private University*
Irv Broughton, *The Blessing Of The Fleet*
Justin Caldwell, *The Sleeping Porch*
Mark Craver, *The Problem Of Grace*
Quinton Duval, *Dinner Music*
Honor Johnson, *Small As A Resurrection*
Frances Mayes, *Hours*
John McKernan, *Walking Along The Missouri River*
John S. Morris, *Bean Street*
Stan Rice, *Body Of Work*
Frank Stanford, *You; The Singing Knives;*
The Battlefield Where The Moon Says I Love You
Carolyn Beard Whitlow, *Wild Meat*

IN TRANSLATION

René Char, *No Siege Is Absolute* versions by Franz Wright
Philippe Soupault, *I'm Lying* transl. by Paulette Schmidt

FICTION

Alison Bundy, *A Bad Business*
Mary Caponegro, *Tales From The Next Village*
Myra Sklarew, *Like A Field Riddled By Ants*
Steve Stern, *Isaac And The Undertaker's Daughter*

ART

Zuleyka Benitez, *Trouble In Paradise*

TRAVEL

Barbara & Sandra Heller, *New Orleans My Darling*